How to Grow Rich by Creating Multiple Streams of Residual Income

By Praveen Kumar

Copyright © 2012   By Praveen Kumar

All Rights Reserved.

Unauthorized distribution or duplication is strictly prohibited

Terms of Use

This book is Copyright © 2011 By Praveen Kumar. All rights are reserved. No part of this book may be reproduced, stored in a retrieval system, or transmitted by any means; electronic, mechanical, photocopying, recording, or otherwise, without written permission from the copyright holder(s).

Disclaimer

The advice contained in this material might not be suitable for everyone. The author obtained the information from sources believed to be reliable and from his own personal experience, but he neither implies nor intends any guarantee of accuracy.

The author, publisher and distributors never give legal, accounting, medical or any other type of professional advice. The reader must always seek those services from competent professionals that can review their own particular circumstances.

The author, publisher and distributors particularly disclaim any liability, loss, or risk taken by individuals who directly or indirectly act on the information contained herein. All readers must accept full responsibility for their use of this material.

All pictures used in this book are for illustrative purposes only. The people in the pictures are not connected with the book, author or publisher and no link or endorsement between any of them and the topic or content is implied, nor should any be assumed. The pictures are only licensed for use in this book and must not be used for any other purpose without prior written permission of the rights holder.

Customer Reviews

5.0 out of 5 stars: Love this book!!!, October 16, 2013

By
mjones28

Verified Purchase

This review is from: **(Kindle Edition)**

This book is an excellent read for anyone looking to make a living on "autopilot. The author speaks of unique ways, not the common topics to make money. I will refer to this book again and again for my money making ideas. I myself, as the author of the book, "A Single Mother, A Few Perspectives, and anyone else that is a single parent" agree that sharing your knowledge and utilizing your talents awaits the true "money maker".

5.0 out of 5 stars: How to Grow Rich by Creating Multiple Streams of Residual Income, June 24, 2013

By
James J. King "king james" (texas)

Verified Purchase

This review is from: **(Kindle Edition)**

What an awesome book. I learned so much about creating multiple streams of passive income that I have started some of the author's suggestions and have begun making money myself.

4.0 out of 5 stars: Very inspirational, April 13, 2013

By
New Mom "New Mom" (Virgin Islands) -

Verified Purchase(What's this?)

This review is from: **(Kindle Edition)**

The book was written in an easy to read and follow format and provided very good ideas that can be explored further. His advice can work for anyone that is willing to put in the work.

5.0 out of 5 stars: Make this simple idea the bedrock of your financial freedom

Most people are financial slaves because they trade their time for freedom. The heart surgeon gets paid a lot more for their time than the McDonald's team member, but the principle is the same.

Freedom lies in creating residual income.

That is, income that continues with little or no additional effort on your part.

March 4, 2012 by Richard Stooker

4.0 out of 5 stars: Has some good concepts, March 12, 2013

By
Mr. J. REDWOOD –

Verified Purchase(What's this?)

This review is from: **(Kindle Edition)**

Good concepts ideas, but doesn't delve too deeply into anything more than that - other than 'make residual income' there are many ways to fail doing this. Recommended quick reading to open you up to a few possibilities.

5.0 out of 5 stars: Great content!, August 16, 2012

By
Jason K (Tacoma WA)

This review is from: **How to Grow Rich by Creating Multiple Streams of Residual Income (Kindle Edition)**

This is truly and excellent book! GREAT content. This isn't just another 'fluff' filled e-book. Quality stuff. I'd highly recommend you read it and act upon it

5.0 out of 5 stars: How to Grow Rich, March 5, 2012

By
George J Barendse

This review is from: **(Kindle Edition)**

Residual income is income that keeps coming in month after month, year after year, from work you do only ONCE. One type of residual income is earned when a product is sold and the customer reorders the same product again and again requiring no additional effort. This type of order is referred to as an auto-ship.

Multiple streams are likely to bring in more revenue and will increase opportunities for residual income. A successful online business is an online business that works for the online business owner through multiple steady flowing streams of income, and what is more important, substantial residual income.

These tips are helpful but to receive complete and comprehensive information, ONLY this Ebook "How to Grow Rich by Creating Multiple Streams of Residual Income " will give you the needed knowledge to become successful ---buy it!

5.0 out of 5 stars: How to Grow Rich by Creating Multiple Streams of Residual Income (How To Create Wealth), March 5, 2012

By
Ashe111 - See all my reviews

This review is from: **(Kindle Edition)**

Another masterpiece by Praveen Kumar, very informative and makes a pleasant reading. I learned a lot from this eBook and I would highly recommend it to anyone who is interested to learn how to create a permanent residual income!

5.0 out of 5 stars: Make this simple idea the bedrock of your financial freedom, March 4, 2012

By
Richard Stooker "Author, Virgin Blood" (Manchester MO) -

Verified Purchase

This review is from: **(Kindle Edition)**

Most people are financial slaves because they trade their time for freedom. The heart surgeon gets paid a lot more for their time than the

McDonald's team member, but the principle is the same.

Freedom lies in creating residual income.

That is, income that continues with little or no additional effort on your part.

I recommend focusing on one residual income business, build it up, and start investing for income when you can afford to do so.

Grace Darby (Oakland, CA)

Verified Purchase

This review is from: **(Kindle Edition)**

I have just finished reading this book and it is an absolute eye opener on how to create long term wealth that will last for generations.

It not only explains the importance of creating residual income that many books teach but also gives practical ideas and steps to on how to create residual income.

I especially liked the chapters on the 'Wrong Way' and the' Right Way' to create multiple streams of income. There are so many foolish people out there who are touting "Get Rich Quick" schemes. This is a well thought out book about creating income sensibly for the long term.

This is a must read book for any one serious about seeking financial freedom as it lays down the blue print for creating long term wealth.

Table of Contents

Introduction 11
The Myth of Job Security 15
What is the Problem with Linear Income? 19
Residual Income – The Holy Grail of Investing 23
    Why is Residual Income Important? 24
    Benefits of Generating Residual Income 25
    Residual/ Passive Income Misnomer 25
Residual Income Generators 27
    Investors 27
    Businesses 27
Categories of Residual Income 31
Investment in Residual Income 35
    Investing Time 35
    Investing Money 36
    Steps to Create Residual Income 37
    Indexed funds 38
    Dollar Cost Averaging 38
Real Estate as Basis of Residual Income 41
    Rate of Return 41
    Investment Risk 42
    Buy Below Market Value 43
    Increase Value of Investment 44
    Financial Leverage 44
    Control over Investment 45
    Real Estate Offers Exceptional Tax Advantages ... 45
Monitoring Your Investment 47

Fluctuations to National Average 48
Great Passive Income Ideas 51
   Start a Bulk Candy Vending Business 51
   Network Marketing 52
   Set up an Automated eBay Business 54
Online Residual Income 55
   Why Build Residual Income on the Internet? 55
Steps to Create an Online Residual Income 57
   Find a Way to Make Money 57
Action Steps to Create Passive Income Online 65
Why Create Multiple Streams of Residual Income? 67
   The Dreaded Product Life Cycle (PLC) 68
   Problems in Creating Multiple Streams of Income 69
   Is Creating Multiple Streams of Income the Right Strategy for You? 70
   The Wrong Way to Create Multiple Streams of Residual Income 71
   The Right Way to Create Multiple Streams of Residual Income 72
   Practical Steps to Creating Multiple Streams of Residual Income 79
Final Thoughts 83
About The Author 85

Introduction

> "Wealth is when small efforts produce big results, Poverty is when big efforts produce small results" - George David

One of the fundamentals of wealth creation is to know that not all income streams are created equal. When you work and are paid only once then your income is linear.

In the case of residual income, you work hard once and it unleashes a steady flow of income for years and maybe even a lifetime or beyond. It is often said that lower and middle class work for money where as the rich make their money work for them. The key to wealth creation lies in this simple statement.

Royalties from Elvis Presley songs and movies earn an income in excess of $40.0 million every year even though he has been dead for over three decades. Although everyone cannot be an Elvis Presley but it is definitely possible to focus on work that will create a residual income rather than spend a lifetime in working for linear income.

Doctors, dentists, sales persons, attorneys may appear to have impressive incomes but they are linear in nature. Their incomes are capped depending upon the number of hours they work. If they don't show up for work due to any reason their income comes to a grinding halt. They trade hours of work for income.

Introduction

This kind of an income is full of potential risks. In case of ill health or an accident, the income dries up immediately. This has dire consequences for the financial wellbeing of the individual and the families. Even if one is insured, the money runs out ultimately and there is a need to downgrade the life style and make adjustments that can be very painful.

The true definition of wealth is the time period for which you can sustain your life style in case you stop working today. If you can sustain your life style for only a few months then it is a cause for serious concern. If you can do it for a couple of years then you are better off. On the other hand if you can sustain your life style indefinitely without work then you can be termed as wealthy. Once you reach this stage you can retire.

It must be remembered that contrary to what many think, you need more money in retirement because now you have all the time in the world to holiday and spend money and also to pay for those extra medical bills. If you are banking on social security or pension as your only residual income source then you are in for serious disappointment.

Almost all of us with the exception of a few very rich people start with a linear income. The smart ones are those who start shifting their incomes from linear to residual from a very young age.

Every day when you wake up you must ask yourself the question 'What percentage of my income is residual?' Also ask yourself 'How many hours am I going to devote today towards creating a residual income'. If you don't ask these questions you will remain where you are.

You are in big trouble if you devote 'Zero' hours towards creating passive income. Remember true wealth is created by focusing on work that creates an income for a lifetime. For every hour of work you put in, you should be paid again and again and not only once as in the case of linear income. Therein lays the secret of wealth creation.

"How many times do you get paid for every hour of work you put in?" The answer to this question will tell you if your income is linear or passive. If you are paid only once for your work then your income is linear. If you don't show up for work you don't get paid. You work from pay check to pay check. When the source of your income is residual you get paid for your effort again and again.

One of the main reasons why people find it difficult to leap from linear or earned income to residual income is that the entire education system is designed to prepare people to get jobs that can pay them salaries. This helps the big businesses to get trained labour for their industries and also works well for the government in collecting tax dollars as paid workers pay the highest amount of tax.

> **"When a Man tells you that he got rich through hard work, ask him "Whose?"**
> Don Marquis

You have to create a shift in your thinking before you can start generating residual income. You have to free yourself from the shackles of the unfortunate education system that has gripped your psychology.

This book will educate you not only on the importance of residual income but also how you can shift gradually from earned income to residual income and find financial freedom for life.

Introduction

The Myth of Job Security

> "A job is really a short-term solution to a long term problem."

People with jobs believe that their 'income' is representative of their wealth. The questions they ask are "who do you work for?" "How much do you earn?" or "what car do you drive?"

These people fall into the category of "looking good, going nowhere". They buy stuff to look and feel rich. To sustain their life style they continually work harder, longer hours and constantly educate themselves to become even more specialized.

A pay check, no matter how big, cannot be defined as wealth or riches. Most people think that getting a bigger pay check or salary is making them richer. Nothing can be further from truth. In fact 95% of people spend every dollar they earn. By the way acronym for job is "Just Over Broke"

We need 'cash flow' to pay our bills, put food on the table, send our kids to school and sustain any kind of life style. But if your 'cash flow' is solely reliant on your pay check then you are at grave risk. You can fall ill, have an accident or lose your job. Ask millions who have lost their jobs in the financial down turn.

The Myth of Job Security

"Job security is a myth...it is also risky for self-employed people in my opinion. If they get sick, injured, or die, their income is directly impacted."...........Robert Kiyosaki

Having a job severely restricts your cash flow capabilities. You can work for only 'X' hours in a day. Your pay check will be limited to number of hours worked multiplied by your hourly rate.

Your first step to creating wealth comes when your 'cash flow' starts coming from passive income rather than pay check. In other words, your investments and businesses pay you money whether you get out of bed or not.

Your next step forward is to create long term passive income cash flow backed by solid asset base. Wealth is all about owning assets. However an asset must have both capital growth and income. Don't buy property first if you want to become rich or you will become 'asset rich' and 'cash poor'. You must first concentrate on generating a rather large passive income. Cash flow not only supports your life style but also has the ability to get loans to buy income producing assets.

Passive cash flow is generated out of investments (paper assets or properties that are fully paid for), businesses that have systems in place and do not require your day to day presence, or your income generated as a result of royalties from intellectual property rights that you have created. To grow rich you have to make either money or people work for you even when you sleep or are holidaying on the beach.

The quickest way to become rich fast is to generate massive cash flow through a business that has proven systems. You then have to buy assets that give you not only passive income but also capital appreciation. If you do not have a huge capital to start a business, then join a good network marketing company. It is not only a good passive income generator but you will also get personalized coaching in business, marketing and leadership skills from those who have stakes in your business.

So every night before you go to sleep calculate the number of hours you have spent in creating passive income for yourself as against the number of hours you have spent in generating linear income that has helped others get rich because of your effort. You must set a target each day to add more and more hours towards generating passive income. If you do this simple exercise on a regular basis you will take a giant leap towards attaining financial freedom.

To understand the difference between residual and linear income is critical to your financial wellbeing. Most people do not understand the distinction and stay in a job for their entire life or run a 'mom-and-pop' business that requires their attention and presence seven days a week. So whenever you are looking at a business or an investment opportunity, look at the residual aspect. If it is not there then give it a miss. Never ever forget the commandment if you want to become truly rich: 'Thou shall work once and be paid for a lifetime'.

The Myth of Job Security

What is the Problem with Linear Income?

The main problem with linear or earned income is that you are trading your time and skills for money. Your earning power will be limited by the time and skills you personally have. This is a very inefficient and arduous way of earning wealth. You have only 'X' number of hours in a day and also there is a limit to the skills you can acquire. These limiting factors will put a cap on your income.

As soon as you stop working or your skills become outdated your income will stop. You can take time out to upgrade your skills but during that period your income levels will either drop or stop altogether.

When it comes to linear income, you are the golden goose. As you grow older your physical and mental capacities get reduced. This will reflect directly on your earned income. In case of ill health or an accident your income will drop to a virtual zero.

Another major issue with earned income is that in virtually every country it is taxed more heavily when compared to investments or residual income. The biggest financial out flow in your life are the taxes. You pay virtually 40% to 70% of your earnings to the government in form of direct and indirect taxes. These include income tax, GST, customs and excise duty, capital gains tax, estate duty, stamp duty, service tax, VAT, property taxes, regional council taxes etc. Some of the indirect taxes are invisible and you don't even come to know about them.

What is the Problem with Linear Income?

Linear or earned income has very limited number of loop holes to save on the taxes. If you are in a job you have to start investing or start a part time business to save on the taxes that will provide you with additional funds to build residual income for you and your family. This may seem unfair but it is true. Most governments want you to invest your money so that capital formulation creates more jobs. This is why they give huge tax breaks to investors and business owners. You should take advantage of these tax breaks to create residual income for yourself.

If earned income has so many drawbacks then why most people seek jobs? The reasons are very simple. Jobs do not require a start-up capital or risk. Most people when starting out in life do not have capital and are risk averse. The fault also lies in our education system which was designed during the industrial age to train people for jobs that the industries run by capitalists required. Things have changed dramatically with the advent of the information age. It is now possible to earn residual income with very little or virtually no start-up capital or risk.

There is no harm in starting up with a job because most of us start with liner income. A job may also be essential for some people because it can instil discipline and teach skills that are required to succeed in life. The trick is to convert your linear income into residual income within the shortest period of time.

Can you become wealthy from earned income? It depends on your definition of wealth. Some professionals like doctors, investment bankers, lawyers and engineers are highly paid. But are they really rich or simply appearing to be rich? Do their jobs provide long term financial security? Can they sustain their life style if they lose their jobs for any reason?

What is the Problem with Linear Income?

According to me, the true secret of wealth is not that you have more money but that you have more time freedom. You do not have to trade your time for earning money. You will be rich when you can not only sustain your life style without working but also improve on it. In this case you have sufficient residual income to not only sustain your life style but also make your wealth grow by further investments into generating passive income.

When you are trading time for money you do not have time freedom. You can definitely become wealthy if you invest a part of your earned income into creating residual income which in course of time can surpass your earned income.

What is the Problem with Linear Income?

Residual Income – The Holy Grail of Investing

Simply put residual income is an income that is not dependent on your time or effort. It is dependent on the asset and management of that asset. You have to leverage other people's time and money to create residual income and manage the asset.

Businesses can be a source of passive income only if you can replace yourself. If you are directly involved in your business on a day to day basis then it cannot be termed as a passive income. To turn your business into a residual income source you have to put the right kind of people and systems into place so that it operates without your presence and interference. Most entrepreneurs start a business idea for them to generate millions but instead land up shackling themselves to their business and can't even afford to take a holiday in years.

The best kind of residual investments are those where you as the owner of the asset can exercise active control even though you are not involved in day to day operation. You must have adequate control over your asset so as to positively impact on the level of generated income.

Using other people's money and resources is the key ingredient of creating residual income. It buys you time and effort. Once you start creating residual income you will start attracting more and more of other people's money to grow even richer. If done correctly you will get caught in an upward spiral of residual wealth creation.

Residual income without doubt is the holy grail of investing and key to long term wealth. This is a critical step on your road to wealth creation. The earlier you begin this journey more is the success that you will achieve. You can create a tidal wave in your financial security and prosperity if you do not waste a day. It is simple and easy. You simply have to make a start and there is no better time than today.

Why is Residual Income Important?

Residual income is important because every dollar you earn from this source is not dependent on your time or effort. Residual income gradually frees up your time to enhance creativity and improve quality of your life. It gives you financial security and improves your relationship with your family members as there are reduced time and finance constraints in your life.

Residual income frees up your time and also gives you tax breaks to give you even more dollars to create residual income. When you understand the residual game and implement it methodically, your income will spiral upwards along with freeing up your time.

You can never become rich on earned income because you are trading time for money. To become truly rich you have to separate your time from the money you earn. Creating wealth does not have to be about extracting last ounce of your energy. If you take a conscious decision you can gradually shift from linear income to generating residual income that will remain with you for generations to come.

Benefits of Generating Residual Income

- Freedom to choose when and where you wish to work

- Residual income is generated 24 hours 7 days a week

- Freedom to create unlimited amount of income only limited by your imagination

- Have time to spend with your family and friends or go on a vacation

- Retire young

- Financial security for your family in case of illness or ill health

- Ability to give to charitable causes dear to your heart

Residual/ Passive Income Misnomer

Before we discuss residual income let me clarify the misunderstanding that has been created by the term 'passive income'. The terms 'residual income' and 'passive income' have become inter changeable but there is a subtle difference. From marketing point of view the term 'passive income' is very seductive as it equates to "No work", "No brainer", "Easy", "Just sit back and relax and money will come rolling in". People get excited and join a business opportunity thinking that there is no work involved. They get disillusioned when they find that the income is not passive after all.

Nothing can be further from truth. To create residual income there can be huge amount of time and effort upfront. It may take an author months or years to write a book. There is no income upfront. But once the book is published royalties from it can flow for years to come giving passive income.

This is why I have titled this book 'How to Grow Rich by Creating Multiple Streams of Residual Income' and not 'passive income' because I do not wish to put 'easy and misleading filters'. Residual implies that some work must be done upfront before you can reap the rewards for years.

There is no such thing as "100% passive income". Every income stream you create will require some effort up front and also some maintenance effort to sustain the passive income. You must keep these two work factors in mind before embarking on creating a passive income stream. So you have to roll up your sleeves and get to work to start a residual income stream.

The good part is that once you have created your residual income stream then it will create a full time income for you with very few hours of work each week. There was a point in my life when I took a decision that I will not devote a single hour of my time in generating linear income and make someone else rich. Within a short period of six months from making that decision, I was earning double the amount of residual money by working just 5 hours a week. Someone rightly said that **"Wealth is not a material gain, but a state of mind."**

You will need some involvement in management of the asset although it may not require day to day direct involvement.

Rich people develop skills of putting systems into place and using other people's time and money. Poor people land up in working for rich people and making them rich through their labor.

Residual Income Generators

Now let us examine some of the passive income generating opportunities. You may use one or a combination of the methods to generate passive income.

Investors

- Real Estate investors get cash flow from rent in addition to capital gain
- Saving Account owners earn interest
- Investors in shares get dividends and appreciation
- Discount mortgagers earn interest
- Tax lien certificate holders earn interest penalties
- Debenture holders earn interest

Businesses

- Entrepreneurs who auto pilot their businesses earn passive profits
- Franchisors get a percentage of gross revenue or profits
- Partners get share of profits

- Venture partners get percentage of profits

Royalties

- Authors get royalties from their books and tapes

- Musicians and song writers get royalties from their work

- Visual artists get royalties from paintings

- Inventors get royalties

- Game designers get royalties

- Actors get a percentage of the profits

Miscellaneous

- Company Pension Plans offer income flow

- Retired persons get pensions

- Network marketers build residual income through leverage

- Corporate managers get stock options

- Insurance agents get residual income from their sales

- Securities agents get residual sales

- Celebrity endorsers get a gross percentage of profits

- Mailing list owners get rental fees

Residual Income Generators

The above list is not exhaustive. It is possible to automate virtually any business by putting in systems and delegating authority. It is also possible to franchise businesses for passive income or sell shares to create wealth. There are always some costs involved. But the effort is worth it because what you will create is something more powerful. You will create income streams that do not need your presence.

The trick is let your money work for you and not you working for money. Once you start generating passive income your money will be working for you night and day even when you sleep.

Residual Income Generators

Categories of Residual Income

For clearer understanding we can divide residual income into two broad categories:

- Residual Income sources that require startup capital or additional fund to maintain and grow

- Residual income sources that require little or no startup capital or maintenance money

The first category will need initial capital from your earned income, family money, funds from investors or borrowed funds from banks to purchase assets that will generate passive income for you. When you borrow money you create debt. This provides you leverage to create accelerated wealth but it also comes with associated risks that can destroy your wealth. For greater understanding of this subject you can read one of my books **'How to Grow Rich with the Power of Leverage'** as this subject is beyond the scope of this book.

Examples of this type of residual income will be investing in stocks & other paper assets, real estate investments or buying businesses that have systems in place that need very little of your personal time to run the company. An example will be a good franchise business like the McDonalds that has systems in place and will need very little intervention on your part.

The second category of residual income requires very little financial out lay and is generated through assets that you create by writing a book, song, software, patent

Categories of Residual Income

or trade mark. Internet has provided a new medium to generate residual wealth through creation of Virtual Real Estate.

Virtual Real Estate is the new gold rush and without doubt it is the new frontier that you have to master to create residual income. Internet is creating new millionaires every minute even as you read this book. What is virtual real estate? These are the assets you create on the internet. These include your websites, domain names, email lists, online businesses, Facebook, Twitter and other social media accounts. Once you create these assets you can generate residual income from them for years.

We will discuss this at greater length later in the book.

You can further categorize residual income into:

- Offline Residual Income

- Online Residual Income

Offline residual income generally requires more capital. You can take advantage of a variety of financial advisers and products to start investing in residual income investment schemes like paper assets and real estate. You can also get bank funding for buying these assets and hence can leverage your time and money.

On the other hand online residual income or creation of Virtual Real Estate requires very little and in some cases no start-up capital. There are many online gurus but no financial advisers. Banks will not fund it because the risks are too high. It is a new frontier of wealth creation that is still in progression. It is still Wild West out there. You have to make the effort to increase your knowledge to create wealth in the new environment. There are many scam artists who will make you part with your hard earned money on the internet. You have to be extremely careful before pulling out your wallet. There are risks but very high rewards as well. Opportunities are endless. If you make the effort of mastering the new environment you can create large amounts of residual income with very little effort in shortest possible time frame.

Creating residual income on the internet does not give you financial leverage but technological leverage. Financial leverage creates debt with associated risks. Technological leverage on the other hand is debt free and faster.

The best instrument to be used to create residual income will depend upon your financial situation, time availability and state of knowledge at a given point. If you have plenty of capital and cash flow from your job or business but no time then it will be better for you to employ services of a professional financial adviser to invest in offline assets such as real estate, stocks, bonds, CDs, commodities like gold, silver etc.

On the other hand if you are internet savvy with little or no capital then creating Virtual Real Estate to generate residual income may be the right choice for you. You have to also take into account your risk appetite for a particular type of investment. Your assessment of your situation is the key to making a successful choice.

Categories of Residual Income

Investment in Residual Income

You will need to make a significant initial investment to create a passive income. This investment can be in terms of money or investment in time.

Investing Time

Most time investing passive incomes comprise of ideas that will need energy inputs as well. Generally, you will be turning your spare time into some sort of product that will provide a steady stream of income over time.

Everyone has some unique knowledge skill that can be converted into electronic books and sold on the internet to create passive income. The beauty of life is that each one of us has a unique experience that can be shared with others in form of blogs and books. This sharing of unique information can be monetized. I've already written several books –**'How to Grow Rich with the Power of Leverage'** and **'How to Grow Rich with the Power Compounding'** to name a few. These books are working for me as passive income generators. I sell hundreds of copies each month and generate a healthy passive income. I am simply sharing my experience with others and creating value in their lives. Each book that I write is a new source of passive income for me.

Publishing books was a problem earlier on as only few big authors were accepted by publishing houses. This is no longer the case. You can now self-publish a book with Kindle, Barnes and Noble, Nook etc. The options for self-publishing are getting better and better with each passing day.

You can also create blogs with the information you wish to share with others and monetize them. Once the blog is in place you will be required to spend some time developing links to it so that Google can find it. After that, your blog or website will keep generating a steady trickle of advertisement and referral revenue.

Investing Money

If you have money to invest then you can simply invest that money into generating passive income for you. You can consider some of the following paper assets to generate passive income:

> • **Dividend-bearing stocks** If you buy let us say $20,000 worth of Coca-Cola shares then you will be entitled to receive regular dividend payments that will give you passive income. Over a period your stock will multiply and gain in value increasing your dividend payments. You should choose a very stable company that pays out a very steady dividend, this type of approach can earn a very reliable income for you. You might also want to invest in mutual funds that are indexed to spread out your investments over a large number of stocks (less risk). I will cover more of this strategy later in the book.
>
> • **Treasury inflation-protected securities (TIPS)** are bonds that you can purchase from the government whose face value adjusts according to the rate of interest, so that when the TIPS matures, you will be able to sell it for more than the initial purchase price. TIPS return is at a very low rate but

they have the advantage of being rock-solid investments that will match inflation growth when you sell them.

- **Savings accounts and CDs** are similar rock-solid investments. They are also very liquid (meaning you can cash out your money whenever you need it). The interest rates are generally on the lower side. There are, however, times when a savings account or CD is very solid.

- **Annuities** are investments you can purchase from an insurance company that will pay you a certain amount of residual income every year for the rest of your life. The younger you are, the smaller will be your contribution. Let's say, for example, that you purchase a $30,000 annuity, one that the insurance house quotes at 4%. It would mean that you would receive $1200 each year for the rest of your life from that company. The risk you have here is that the insurance company may eventually become insolvent, leaving you with nothing at all. You must therefore seek out an insurance company with a long history of stability and good bond rating. You must also diversify across multiple insurance houses.

Steps to Create Residual Income

In most cases people start out in jobs as their primary source of income. You have to start using a part of your actively earned income into generating passive income on a regular basis. You will be surprised how fast your residual income will grow if you start out early enough. Your investments will multiply if you apply the power of compounding properly. A dollar a day if invested correctly will make you a millionaire before you retire.

I have written a very interesting book on this subject that I strongly recommend that you read it. It is titled **'How to Grow Rich with the Power of Compounding'**. Most of us learnt about compound interest at school. We also did a few sums but no one ever explained to us either its power or application. Our teachers and parents would be millionaires if they understood or had any comprehension of its awesome power. This book will teach you how to apply its awesome power to your advantage.

If you are new to the stocks and mutual funds then I will advise you to go for investing in indexed funds using Dollar Cost Averaging. This strategy gives highest returns with minimum amount of risk. Let me explain:

Indexed funds

Indexed funds are type of mutual funds with a portfolio constructed to match or track the components of a market index, such as the Standard & Poor's 500 Index (S&P 500). An index mutual fund provides broad market exposure and low operating expenses as no fund manager is involved. The lack of active management generally gives the advantage of lower fees and lower taxes in taxable accounts. This increases your returns as an investor. It has been found that indexed funds out perform funds managed by fund managers as there is no human intervention and mistakes.

Dollar Cost Averaging

This technique involves buying a fixed dollar amount of a particular investment on a regular schedule, regardless of the share price. More shares are purchased when prices are low, and fewer shares are bought when prices are high. Eventually, the average cost per share of the security will become smaller and smaller. Dollar-cost averaging lessens the risk of investing a large amount in a single investment at the wrong time. No financial expert has been able to predict the behavior of stock market accurately.

Dollar cost averaging will reduce your risk considerably. In dollar cost averaging you will need to decide on three parameters: the fixed amount of money invested each time, the investment frequency, and the time horizon over which all of the investments are made. The longer the time horizons the better are the results. The minimum recommended period is 12 months.

The best way to start building residual income is to combine investing in indexed mutual funds using dollar cost averaging strategy. This way you will get the highest returns with minimum risk. Many fund managers will advise you against this strategy because they do not benefit from it. Take the human element out of investing. Let the market magic work. It has shown time and again that index funds beat the performance of most fund managers. The exception to the rule is Warren Buffet! If you can find a fund manager backed with 20 years track record of beating the market then go for it. I have yet to find one.

Investment in Residual Income

Real Estate as Basis of Residual Income

Once you have built some capital then start investing in real estate. Why must you invest in property? This is because real estate investment has produced more self-made millionaires in history than any other instrument of investment. This may change in the near future because of the internet revolution that has started churning out new millionaires in hoards. But you can't beat the solidity of real estate when it comes to creating residual income and long term wealth.

You have to understand how real estate compares with other investment avenues such as savings account, shares/stocks, commodities &; businesses.

Rate of Return

Return on investment (ROI) is definitely one of the most important criteria you should consider whilst taking an investment decision. However simplistic calculations based on yields can be very misleading.

Yield by definition is the ratio of the annual income generated by the investment divided by the dollar amount of investment.

Rate of return should be considered after taking into account the risk involved, whether the investment is inflation adjusted, is there any capital growth on the principal invested, does the investment provide tax benefits and is it possible to leverage your money to get higher returns.

Real estate investments when compared to bank deposits are definitely superior in terms of yield and capital appreciation. Savings in bank do not provide hedge against inflation and your money depreciates in value over a period of time.

Shares and stocks are perceived to have higher returns than property and provide hedge against inflation but they pale in comparison to real estate when you take into account the leveraging power of real estate investing and tax advantages of property. It is possible to buy properties by using Other People's Money (OPM) with returns that are 20 or 30 or 50 or 100 percent or more per annum.

Investment Risk

Banks are perceived to have the least risk when compared to other investments but of late this confidence has been shattered due to the high rate of failure of the banks.

Stocks carry a much higher risk because their values fluctuate on a minute to minute basis. Stocks also do not go up in value and business disasters like Enron can have a nasty effect on your stock market wealth plan.

Investing in businesses can be very profitable if you know what you are doing. The failure rate of new start-up businesses is around 80%. In business you invest in people and ideas which are usually not as solid as bricks and mortars.

Property on the other hand goes up in value slowly and steadily. This is proven by the record of past 300 hundred years where property values have consistently doubled every 8 to 12 years. In the market crash of 2008-2009 when the stocks nose-dived to 50% to 80% of their value and wiped out the fortunes of millions of people, the real estate prices went down by 5% to 30% of their value.

If you wish to understand risk then just check what banks are willing to lend their money for. Are they willing to loan money to buy paintings, antiques, diamonds, mutual funds, CDs, commodities, stocks & businesses? If so to what level of funding is available? For properties banks will easily lend to 70 or 80 or 90 per cent and in some cases to even 100 per cent of the value. Banks are the most risk adverse institutions and if they are willing to invest in real estate up to 100% of value then they consider the investment risk to be extremely low when compared to other investments. You should take your cue from the banks.

Buy Below Market Value

You must have heard the saying that 'you make money when you buy' and not at the time of selling. Is it possible to buy stocks or diamond or commodity or gold below value? When you buy $100,000 worth of stock you pay $100,000 in cash.

Investing in real estate after gaining a bit of knowledge, you can buy properties that are 10 or 20 per cent or even more below market value. There are many reasons why people sell their properties below value. You can amass great wealth by simply buying property below market value.

Increase Value of Investment

Can you increase the value of your stock or bank deposit by tinkering with it? There is simply no mechanism by which you can increase the value of your stock or any other investment because you do not control them. However you can greatly increase the market value of your investment property by spending a small amount of money on making cosmetic changes or applying for change of use of the property.

Financial Leverage

No one has ever become rich without applying the power of leverage. Archimedes rightly stated in 200 BC that '**Give me a lever long enough and a place to stand and I will move the entire earth**.'

The financial leverage in the investment world comes from the use of OPM or Other People's Money. In real estate investing we buy property with 10% down payment and yet we control 100% of real estate.

For example let us say we buy a property of $100,000 with $10,000 down payment. Let us assume that rent from the property covers the mortgage payments and the out goings. If the price of the property moves up by 10% during the year the market value will increase to $110,000. This means we would have made a profit of $10,000 on our investment of $10,000. This is a 100% return on investment and was made possible only because of the power of leverage.

Our return on investment would have been infinity had we bought the property with no down payment. This kind of financial leverage is only possible if you invest in real estate. But before you rush to buy your property with no money down you must understand how leverage works. There is no greater leverage in life than the leverage of knowledge.

It is extremely difficult to finance other types of investments such as stock and businesses because funding is always an issue. Banks love property because of the low risk and capital appreciation associated with real estate.

Leverage can be used for quick wealth creation. If you know how to use leverage you do not need large amounts of initial capital to start your real estate investment portfolio.

Control over Investment

When you invest in stocks you have no control over your investment until and unless you have the controlling shares in a company. You can hand over your money to a fund manager but you still do not have any control and are at mercy of the competence or incompetence of the fund manager.

Shakespeare rightly said *'fool and his money are soon parted'*. There are many Madoffs in this world are waiting to rip you off your hard earned money.

Invest in real estate and you have full control over your asset. You are not at someone else's mercy that can part with your money. You control the shots and have peace of mind.

Real Estate Offers Exceptional Tax Advantages

The biggest expense in your lifetime is the taxes you pay to the government. I must repeat once again. You will find that you pay in excess of 50% you earn to the government in the form of taxes. Most people are not even aware of how much they pay because some taxes are indirect taxes.

Rich are rich because they pay little or no taxes. If you are smart you can do the same and fund your life style and investments by saving on the taxes.

Real estate tax laws differ from one country to another. However, universally applied tax principles throughout the Western world hugely favour those who invest in properties. As opposed to other investments, you can run your property investment as a business and claim back depreciation, interest payments and other expenses as a part of your business.

It is sufficient to say that tax refunds from real estate investments provide you with additional cash flow to buy more investment properties and create residual income.

In case of stocks and shares you have virtually no tax benefits and have to pay tax on interest and dividends received.

This unique advantage makes investing in real estate very attractive when compared to other investment opportunities.

Monitoring Your Investment

The whole point of investing is to create multiple streams of residual income that can fund your life style. There is no fun if you have to monitor your investment on an hourly or day to day basis which is the case with investments in stocks, foreign currency or commodities, the values of which change constantly. You have to watch these investments like a hawk if you have to succeed.

Property prices tend to move very slowly, smoothly and constantly with minimum amount of fluctuations. This makes it very easy to monitor your real estate investment.

My philosophy is very simple. I buy real estate at 10 to 20 per cent below market value. I then make improvements to increase the value of the property and make it cash flow positive. I then hand over the property to a competent property manager. Once I complete a project I move on to the next one.

After the initial investment of time and energy, there is very little of my personal involvement in the property. There are at times months or even years before I need to actively intervene in a property as it runs on auto pilot. I treat every property as an individual business centre and source of passive income. I set up my properties in such a way that they require virtually no monitoring from me apart from going through the monthly statement of accounts.

Invest in real estate and you will have the most passive and hands free of all the investments opportunities.

Fluctuations to National Average

The price of each stock fluctuates on its own merit and there are numerous imponderable variables that dictate the price of a stock. It is therefore very difficult to monitor every stock in your portfolio because each one is very different from the other. It requires a genius of Warren Buffet calibre to beat the market averages consistently. Even expert fund managers struggle to keep up with market averages.

In the case of real estate, fluctuations of any one property relative to the national average are very low. It requires very little expertise to beat the national average for property and increase your return on investment.

Real estate investment is very forgiving to mistakes. It is the simplest, most reliable, most consistent and hassle free vehicle to convert even a little bit of financial intelligence into cold hard cash. This is the reason why you must invest in real estate.

Real Estate is without doubt the safest way to create long term residual income.

Many people buy property with the hope of creating passive cash flow in order to retire. Sometimes they get disappointed because their properties do not generate adequate cash flow to retire even after they have bought 5 to 10 properties. The problem arises because they buy negatively geared properties that are highly leveraged. In order to create residual income you have to buy cash flow properties and reduce your mortgage over a period of time.

Monitoring Your Investment

Properties take time to create residual income. As time goes by the prices and rents go up. These two factors will increase your equity and cash flow. You can also convert equity into cash flow to create residual income.

Also do not confuse property, forex, commodity or share trading as instruments for creating residual income. These are nothing but full time jobs with little or no chance of building an asset or generating residual cash flow. These activities are nothing but skill-based jobs on which you have to work full time to make money.

Monitoring Your Investment

Great Passive Income Ideas

There are hundreds of ways in which you can create passive income. We have discussed paper assets and real estate. We will discuss internet marketing in the next chapter. In this chapter we will discuss some offline business ideas that are easy to implement.

Start a Bulk Candy Vending Business

You must have seen vending machines in cinema halls or lobby of hotels and restaurants. Have you wondered who owns these machines? Most of these machines are owned by independent business entrepreneurs who have negotiated to place the machines with the parent business owner either by paying a fixed rent or giving them share of the profits.

Vending machines business needs small initial investment. It has very low maintenance cost and provides excellent return on investment. Its success depends upon finding good secure locations.

This is an excellent way to start building your residual income if you do not have large capital or do not qualify for a loan to start buying real estate. The difficult part of this business is to find good locations. You may have to knock on several doors before you secure your first location. Once you are in business and have built a good profile it will become relatively easy to find and secure new locations.

Network Marketing

Network marketing is perhaps the most misunderstood and the most controversial concept of passive wealth creation. It generates strong emotions. Most of us were invited to a fancy presentation and got excited with the prospect of working from home, firing our boss, no office politics or commuting to work. There was also no cap on the income potential.

The prospect of generating great amount passive income excited us as it would give us time with our families, travel the world and pursue our other fantasies. It was better than any retirement plan or job security. It could be started part time with minimal start-up costs. There were dreams in our eyes of a better future. But then what happened.... reality broke through. We suffered rejection from our friends and families. Our recruiting drive never took off. We never saw those fancy checks coming into our bank accounts.

On the other hand there are people generating great amounts of passive income through their efforts in network marketing. Network marketing is an industry that is experiencing an exponential growth with turnover of billions of dollars and over 55 million distributors worldwide. It is being taught as a subject in many business schools around the globe. People like Warren Buffet and Donald Trump who are not only some of the richest people on the planet but also have the most astute business minds own direct selling companies.

Richard Bronson who owns over 300 companies worldwide is involved in network marketing. Robert Kyosaki, the author of 'Rich Dad Poor Dad' book series and one of the greatest financial educators recommends network marketing as the 'Perfect Business' to achieve financial freedom and security. Why are these business leaders staking their name and fame to promote a business model that has generated s much debate and negativity? They believe network marketing is the wave of the future.

Many highly respected companies such as AT&T, Direct TV, Gap, Google, Macy's, Nordstrom, Travelocity, and tons more have started to borrow from the concepts of network marketing. These companies have realized that the impact of their multi-million dollar advertising budget pales in comparison to the power of word-of-mouth advertising.

What most people do not realize is that how far network marketing industry has evolved. Network marketing is a relationship building and mentoring business. To succeed you have to build a network of strong relationships and train your distributors to replicate the business model. Internet has made these tasks easier. You no longer have to drive long distances to meet people. You can use 'skype' or send webinar recordings to give product demonstration.

There is big residual income to be made in network marketing. Make no mistakes about it. It is a low investment business model that gives huge returns if you do it properly and sustain your effort. A large part of my income that has helped me to retire and work from home comes from network marketing. The best network marketing businesses that I have found are the ones based on profit sharing principle with the parent company wherein you make money even if you do not sponsor anyone. When people see you making money they join your network without the need of much persuasion. I have also written a book explaining this business model '**The 30 Minute Workweek**'.

Automated eBay Business

If you can source a reliable wholesale product then you have over 50 million customers on eBay to whom you will be able to market your product to. You can fall into the trap of making your eBay business into a full time day job. To create residual income you have to automate the whole process. There are hundreds of software programs available to automate the eBay auctions.

The software will automatically start a new auction as soon as an item sells. It will do everything for you except ship the product. Even shipping of products can be outsourced to make it complete hands off business that generates residual income for you.

The key to success and profit from eBay business is to source the right product to sell. You can buy these products at a huge discount from eBay itself from the "Wholesale Lots" section. You can then turn around and sell them one at a time for a profit.

Online Residual Income

Internet is the new gold rush and without doubt it is the new frontier that you have to master in order to create residual income with minimum amount of investment of time and money. This is a revolution happening right before your eyes with new millionaires being created even as you read this book. It is just the beginning of the new wave of wealth creation. Such unique opportunity happens only once or twice in your lifetime. You will have to grab this opportunity with both hands or will regret for rest of your life.

Why Build Residual Income on the Internet?

The reason why you must start building residual income using internet is because it is revolutionizing the way we think, work and shop.

- It is the most Powerful Media much bigger than television

- It is the Biggest Market Place

- It is the Most Profitable Business

- It is Getting Bigger Every Day

- Internet Business Never Stops 24 hours 365 days

- Requires Very Little Investment and hence No Risk

- It has created more Millionaires and Billionaires than any other opportunity

- It is for Everyone

- You can automate your business very easily to create residual income

There was over $200,000,000,000 in sale over the internet last year. This figure is growing exponentially each and every year. Even if you are able to capture 1/1,000,000 part of this business your earnings will $200,000 per year. How many shares are you prepared to capture?

Once you build your build your internet income it will provide you with passive income and freedom of time to travel the world in style, meet people and share your ideas.

Steps to Create an Online Residual Income

Find a Way to Make Money

There are hundreds of ways to make money on the Internet. Your aim is to find a business that can be automated easily.

Some of the methods you can use are:

Affiliate Marketing

This is passive income derived from setting up a blog or website that pre sells a company's products. You provide reviews and information that drives traffic to your affiliate link. You get paid by the company if someone buys the product from your affiliate link. The trick is to find products that are not only popular but pay good re-occurring commissions. This will create a monthly residual income for you once a sale is made. One such example is selling a monthly subscription to a membership site. Also find products that pay multi-tier commissions. You will then get paid if your affiliate makes a sale.

You must also look at the sales page of the product you are promoting. If the sales page of the product you are promoting is not a good one then your conversion rate will be poor. This means that if you refer 1000 visitors to a sales page through pre-selling on your website and only a handful convert then your effort will be in vain. If a sales page converts well then you will make more money for the same amount of effort.

One example of a great affiliate product is the 'Site Build It' program offered by Ken Envoy. Firstly the product is excellent and gives residual income. In addition the affiliate program offers a number of great products with high commissions with excellent sales materials and content to help you pre sell his products. I **built a website** selling this program which converts very well.

Information Products

People search the internet to find information or solution to their problems. They may be looking for information on weather, health issues, travel information, holiday destinations, cheap tickets, relationship problems, how to make money or how to fix a problem. Human appetite for information is limitless. They also come on the internet for socializing, fun and recreation. You can create information products to satisfy these needs. You can create a report or a book to help them solve their problem and sell it on the internet.

What are the Benefits of Creating an e-Book?

- **Low cost** – The cost of creating an e-Book is extremely low. Once you set up the website with a good sales page you can make sales 24 hours 7 days a week for years to come. You can also take advantage of Clickbank or self-publishing platforms to market your books.

- **Books are Easy to Create** – All you need is an e-Book creation software. You can create a short report or a book in a few days. A large book may take few months or years to write. It is better to create short e-Books of 30 to 40 pages with no fluff. You must write a book to the point and on subjects that people are searching on the internet.

• **Add an Affiliate Program** – It is easy to add an affiliate program to increase sales of your book by sharing the sales revenue with people who promote your book. This will greatly increase your residual income.

• **Promote Affiliate Links** - You can promote affiliate links of related products from within the book to increase your residual income even further. In this book I have added links to some of my other books that are not only relevant but will also provide value addition the reader of the book.

• **Resale Rights** – You can charge a fee for allowing resale rights to people. Once they buy the resale rights they will be able to sell the book and keep 100% of the profits. The advantage to you in this arrangement is that you get to keep the affiliate links inside the books and if a sale takes place then you get to keep the profits.

• **Free e-Books** – Anything free on the internet gets downloaded very fast and goes viral. Writing a free e-Book with affiliate links inside the book is a great way of creating residual income. It is so great that you will not be able to stop your residual income even if you want to stop it once your e-Book goes viral.

Creating Software Products

You don't have to be a software engineer to create a software product. All you need is a great idea of what people want to do faster and easier.

The best example is Bill Gates who created the Windows Operating System. Everyone who has a PC needs it. You could do the same on a smaller scale.

Once you have an idea you can go to a software developer to develop that product for you. If you don't know any software engineer to execute the job then you can go to elance.com or guru.com and post your requirement. Software developers will give their quotes and you can hire one of them after determining their credentials.

You get paid to solve the problems. The bigger the problem your software can solve more you can charge the people. Start by solving small problems and then graduate into developing software for more complex problems.

There are plenty of problems in this world that need solving. I am a real estate investor. I use software for analyzing properties, accounting for my properties, calculating depreciation rates, making presentations to the bank for getting loans, analyzing cost of mortgage, managing tenants & checking if rents are paid. I pay for the software which someone has developed. I need these software for saving time.

Some of the software I use do not have the functions that I need. Here is an opportunity for me to create new software with enhanced functions that will help other property investors who are facing similar problems.

If you look into your daily life you will be able to analyze what functions you need to automate to reduce your workload. You can develop software to automate those functions and market it. But before you start developing a software check in the market place if such software with the functions you need is available otherwise you will be re-inventing the wheel.

Creating software will not give you a residual income. You will have to learn the skill to market the software. Clickbank is a great place to start because it is a market place where you can recruit hundreds if not thousands of affiliates to promote your software product on profit sharing basis.

Advertising Income

You can generate residual advertising income from your website if you have organic traffic coming from search engines. You can offer advertising or banner space to various advertisers for a fee or revenue sharing. Some great programs on the internet are Google AdSense, Infolink, Chitika and Banners Brokers.

The trick here is to create a niche website with great content and build backlinks so that search engines not only find your website but also rank you high in the search engines. This will drive traffic to your website. Your residual income will increase in direct proportion of the traffic to your website.

You can also generate advertising income by allowing placement of ads in your Newsletters or Ezines and e-Books.

Create Membership Site

You can create a membership site and charge a monthly membership fee for accessing information on your website if you are an expert in a field. People will pay for your knowledge, resources you offer and the support you provide. The more members you gain the more residual income you make. You can increase membership of your site by offering an affiliate program wherein you share your monthly revenue with people who bring in new members to your site.

Because you are an expert in your field, you can also recommend other affiliate products and services to your members, from which you earn commissions.

There are excellent software programs on the internet that will help you create a membership site in days.

Pay Per Click Campaigns

You can earn a good passive income by setting up a Pay Per Click campaign using Google Adwords program for some high paying popular affiliate products that are in demand. Once you set up a campaign successfully you can generate excellent passive income from it. I will not recommend this program for a newbie on the internet who does not have good knowledge of Google Adwords. You can lose a lot of money if the adword campaign is not set up correctly.

Before jumping into PPC adwords you should take the trouble of educating yourself on how to set up a successful campaign. One of the most popular books on the subject is 'Advanced Google Adwords' by Brad Geddies. When starting out you should experiment with a small budget. Once a campaign is successful and starts generating profits you can increase your budget and your profits.

I have covered only a few strategies of generating residual income on the internet. There are many more like becoming a reseller, income from referrals, auto blogging etc. Email marketing can be source of passive income once you have created a large email subscriber list. There is very little investment required to generate residual income on the internet and hence there is very little risk. It also gives you time and movement flexibility. You can operate and monitor your business from anywhere in the world where there is an internet connection. In addition the whole world is your market place. You can sell your product anywhere around the globe.

It takes time and effort to master this medium but once you get it right, there is minimum amount of effort involved in generating passive income of your dreams. The trick is to master one strategy properly and it can provide you with residual income to retire. Most people fail because they tend to lose focus and jump from one opportunity to another. When it comes to the internet one can get distracted easily because it has so much to offer in terms of information, entertainment and social interaction.

Steps to Create an Online Residual Income

Action Steps to Create Passive Income Online

I have discussed various residual income opportunities but nothing will come of them if you don't take action. You have to do independent research based on your knowledge and passion. Find a business that is best suited to your temperament and situation. You can convert your knowledge and passion into dollars. Don't fake it be real. Each one of us is born with some unique talent and we experience life in a manner that is also unique to us. We have to share this unique experience with others to earn money on the internet.

Next you must find a business model to share your unique knowledge, talent and experience. Because we are interested in generating residual income, focus on a business opportunity that can be automated. Buy the best product that teaches you the technique. Then simply focus and don't stop till the money starts to flow in.

Action Steps to Create Passive Income Online

Why Create Multiple Streams of Residual Income?

The rich people do not depend on only one source of income, but grow orchards of "money trees."

The famous Nile is the longest river on planet earth. If you look down from a space craft orbiting the earth you will be able see it and its 2 main tributaries quite clearly. It is that big and long. But what you can't see from outer space is all of the thousands of little streams and rivers that run into the Nile. It is all that water from thousands of small streams that pour into the Nile making it so large and invincible.

If you examine the rich you will find that their income is like the river Nile. They have several streams of income pouring in from different sources to create a huge cash flow of residual wealth.

"Prosperous people have always known...If one stream dries up, they have many more to tap into for support. So-called ordinary people are much more vulnerable. If they lose one of their streams, it wipes them out...In the future, you will need a portfolio of income streams -- not one or two, but many streams from completely different and diversified sources -- so that if one stream empties, you'll barely notice. You'll be stable. You will have time to adjust. You will be safe."

The primary benefit to multiple streams of income is the consistency and security of your income coming from non-related sources.

The Dreaded Product Life Cycle (PLC)

Every product or business has what's known as a "Product Life Cycle." Each and every product or business goes through the following four phases:

- Market introduction stage
- Growth stage
- Maturity stage
- Saturation and decline stage

What effect this has on your effort to create residual income? Your residual income source is either growing or dying. Some residual income steams will last through your lifetime but some may dry up pre-maturely. It is great to enjoy the benefits of a residual income stream for the period it lasts. But eventually outside factors will decrease the profits. Eventually every residual income stream that you create will go away forever. Nothing lasts forever. It is the law of life.

I am a great believer in the power of residual income. But one has to be a realist. Eventually the residual income flow you create will disappear one day. This is why it is important to create multiple sources of residual income. If you create large number of income streams they will be in different phases of growth, maturity and saturation stage. All your income streams will not dry out at once. Your cash flow will continue uninterrupted.

Even as you are enjoying benefits of one residual income stream you should be in search of new residual income streams. These are known as "**growth activities**." Once you create a residual income stream its maintenance will take very little of your time. You have to use your time creatively by engaging in growth activities to multiply your residual income streams.

> *"The key to wealth and happiness in today's world is to create multiple streams of income using diverse models and combination of passive and active income in areas where your passions and talents can be most thoroughly engaged."*

Problems in Creating Multiple Streams of Income

The concept of creating financial security through multiple streams of residual income is very appealing. You diversify your investment and business risk. However, when people jump into trying to build multiple streams of income without adequate preparation or thought, reality hits their face. The idea may be great but the problem lies in its successfully implementation. Instead of creating a relaxed life style they get sucked into a situation where they have to become hyper active in trying to control and maintain their residual income sources.

The reality is that we live in a highly competitive and fast changing world. To succeed in any business you need highly specialized knowledge. It is extremely difficult to compete in widely varying fields without adequate skilled knowledge.

Why Create Multiple Streams of Residual Income?

"It is better to have a permanent income than to be fascinating"
Oscar Wilde

We are also limited by time to implement different business strategies. There is also a need to balance our family, health, relationships, recreation and spiritual needs. Happiness lies in balancing our needs correctly rather than focus only on one aspect of life. Financial security is extremely important but it must not be allowed to dominate every aspect of our lives.

Financial success comes from focused attention to one specific outcome. The effort in creating multiple streams of income diffuses your focus and creates extra ordinary demands on your limited time. It can cause undue strain and stress on your life. Your chances of failure increase in proportion to your defused focus. In order to succeed in creating multiple streams of residual income you have to learn to reconcile two seemingly contradictory realities of how to focus and also create multiple streams of income at the same time.

Most people find it extremely difficult to build one stream of residual income successfully during their lifetime. How can they be expected to create multiple streams of income? Let us examine this idea a bit further.....

Is Creating Multiple Streams of Income the Right Strategy for You?

Creating multiple streams of income is not suited to everyone. You must ask yourself the following questions to check if the strategy is right for you:

- Do you have the right knowledge and experience?

- Do you know the principles of time and technology leverage?

- Do you have any previous business or investing experience?

- Do you have a team of experts who can advise and assist you to create multiple streams of income?

- How important are multiple streams of income to you? Are you ready to commit your time and energy to create multiple streams of residual income?

Remember each income stream you create will need its own set of skills, expertise and experience. It will make demands on your time, energy and resources. You will need to pay a price in creating each multiple income stream. Are you willing to pay the price?

The Wrong Way to Create Multiple Streams of Residual Income

The wrong way to create multiple streams of income is to get all fired up and start buying stocks, investing in real estate or jumping into internet businesses without any knowledge or preparation. This is a sure way to failure because you will spread your resources thin and cause undue strain on your system.

You have to learn to walk first and then run or you will fall flat on your face. When you are in the game of money you can destroy your wealth quickly because in each field of wealth creation you will be competing against experts. These people live and breathe in the space they have created. You will need to become an expert before you can compete successfully.

It is fairly simple and easy to create multiple streams of income if you go about it systematically. It is a tough game but it can be made simple if you take the trouble of learning the ropes.

It is not a smart strategy to take undue risk. You can eliminate risk only through acquisition of right skills and knowledge. If you don't have that knowledge then you should be either be willing to pay for that knowledge or team up with people who have the expertise.

The Right Way to Create Multiple Streams of Residual Income

You can maximize your chances of success by taking the following steps:

Step 1: Become an Expert in One Stream

Select your first income stream with great care. This should be based in a field that you have knowledge in and are passionate about. This can be real estate, business, paper assets or internet income. These are broad categories. It will be difficult for you to master the broad category. Within each category there are sub-categories. For instance in real estate you can become an expert in - apartment flats or buildings, single family homes, foreclosure properties, retail shops, industrial properties, office flats or buildings, motels, hotels, buying rundown buildings and making improvements, flipping properties etc. The list is endless. Each sub category requires its own skills.

You will also need to focus on a geographical area. It is impossible to master more than one area. You have to know about the demographics, prices of properties, facilities, transportation & schools in the area, good neighborhoods, real estate agents etc. The list again is endless. Only when you are familiar with an area will you be able to buy a property below its value. Remember profits are made when you buy and not when you sell a property.

In my case I started building my residual income through real estate. My strategy was very simple. My aim was to get a minimum of 10% return from the property. The normal rate of return (ROI) for a single family home in Auckland, New Zealand where I was investing was between 5% to 6%. This was well below my stated goal. I focused on single family homes that had additional land on it to construct a second house. I would try and find a property that was selling at least 15% to 20% below market value. This would give an initial return of around 7% on my investment and also give me instant equity. To increase my rate of return I would construct a second house on the property without sub-dividing the property. This was because sub-division costs were around $60,000 and this expense would not add to my rate of return. My aim was not to sell the second house but to increase my return on investment.

The rent from construction of second house on the property normally increases my return to over 10%. The act of constructing the second house would also increase the valuation of the property by 20%. The fact that I bought the property below market valuation and added value to it by constructing a second house increases my equity over 30% in the property. I then go to the bank and use my equity to buy a second house and repeat the same process again. It takes me around 6 months to complete one project.

Once a project is completed I hand over the property to a competent property manager. From then on it becomes a hand off operation with residual cash flowing from it. My only intervention is to check receipt of my rents every month or once in a while give decision on a major maintenance issue that will cost me more than $500. There are times when I do not speak with my property for months or even a year. By getting 10% return I ensure that the property will become not only self-supporting (pay for the all its expenses, mortgage and management costs) but also give me residual cash flow every week.

I never ever manage my properties or the income stream cannot be termed residual. There are people who try and manage properties themselves and then cry foul about the headache of managing tenants. My property managers do a better job than me. I pay them 6% of the gross rental but this is an expense. In effect I pay them only 4% because of the tax rebate. My vacancy rates are much lower than when I was managing my properties. I have calculated that if my property manager can reduce vacancy by one week in a year then they cost me nothing and pay for themselves. I have properties that are being managed so efficiently that I have not had one day of vacancy in over 7 years.

I treat each property as a separate business centre and an independent source of residual income stream for me. I have repeated this simple formula several times over. After years of doing it successfully I had to abandon this strategy because of increase in Council fees and construction prices. Nothing lasts forever. But as long as it lasted I managed to buy several properties that give me residual income till date.

Once the strategy I described was no longer feasible I started finding large houses in key locations that could be converted into room by room rentals for young professionals. The game goes on.

Step 2: Systemize the First Income Stream

Once you have created your first income stream you must automate your income stream so that it does not require intervention on day to day basis. There will be some maintenance required but if you put proper systems into place then the time required for maintenance can be minimized.

In the example stated in Step 1 above, the simple fact of finding a good property manager made my income stream residual. Every property manager is not equal but with some experience, proper research and interviewing you can find property managers who will take all the headaches of property management from you. This is true for any business. There is saying that you must find a jockey first before buying a business.

You will need either good managers or technology to automate your business operations to create residual income for you. You have to find the right managers, business systems and also invest in right technology to back them up.

You have to master the skills of systemizing your business and investments in order to generate income streams that do not require your presence.

Step 3: Leverage Your First Income to Create Additional Streams of Residual Income

Remember your first income stream is the most important one because you are going to leverage your knowledge and resources from this stream to build other income streams.

Once you have systemized your first income stream you will free up your time to create a second residual income stream. The second residual income stream you create has to be intelligently leveraged out of knowledge, skills and experience gained out of the first income stream. Do not try and create a totally new income stream.

The second income stream may just be a repeat process of the first income stream. You can now make improvements based on your experience in creating the first income stream. You will also need lesser time, effort and money because of your experience. The returns from your second income stream will normally be much higher than your first venture.

Repeat the process again and again till such time market conditions do not change. Once you hit on a successful residual income formula just keep refining and repeating it. Creating residual income can at times be a very boring process. The money part is of course very exciting. Be warned.....human mind wants excitement. It will ask you to try out new ventures and divert your resources from the project that is creating new multiple streams of income. You have to resist this temptation and keep focused on repeating and maximizing your success formula.

A stage will come when you will need to branch out and create new streams of residual income because you can't risk putting your entire income source in one basket. This should be done without changing your field of expertise.

For example in the real estate the example given above my expert field is real estate investment. I have created several streams of residual income by mastering a formula which involved buying a single family home and adding a minor dwelling to it so as to increase my rental return and valuation of the property. Once the Auckland market got saturated I had a choice of repeating the same formula in another town close by where the market conditions are still favorable to that venture.

Why Create Multiple Streams of Residual Income?

To further leverage my knowledge and expertise in real estate investing I created a website that provides free information to visitors on real estate investing. I even offer a free e-Book to help new investors to get them started. Before they download the e-book they have to fill up a form detailing their email address and name. This information is captured in an auto responder that allows me to stay in contact with my list on permission based email marketing. I provide them valuable information regularly.

Sometimes I recommend products that have helped me with my real estate business. My list buys products that I recommend from time to time because they trust me. You must have heard the term that "money is in the list". It is very true. Once you have a large mailing list with whom you have established a relationship of trust you can virtually earn money at will by sending an email recommending a product that will be of value to them. One such email can earn you thousands of dollars.

In addition my website earns money from Infolink and Chitika advertising with whom I have a tie up. Visitors also buy affiliate products from my website. The residual income from my website comes 24/7 without any intervention on my part.

I can further leverage my expertise by writing a book about how I am making money with my real estate investing by giving practical examples from my experience. I am currently working on this book.

If I want I can further leverage my expertise by starting a mentoring program and going on lecture tours. Although these activities cannot be strictly termed as residual income but they can establish me as an authority in my field. The direct fall out can be increased book sales and visitors to my website that will generate even more residual income.

Why Create Multiple Streams of Residual Income?

I have given my example just to illustrate that how you can create multiple streams of income originating from single source of expertise. You can apply this strategy to any field of expertise or are passionate about that you possess.

As you branch out into new residual income streams within your own field of expertise you will need to learn additional skills like learning how to build a website/blog, email marketing, driving traffic to your website, writing a book etc. You can branch out these activities to experts if you have the money and want to achieve quicker results.

Robert Kiyosaki, bestselling author of "Rich Dad Poor Dad", got out of the rat race through real estate before adding paper assets and leveraging the financial knowledge he gained from his investment business experience into a successful information publishing business.

Robert G Allen got out of the rat race through paper assets before leveraging his investing knowledge into real estate and then re-leveraging that same skill set into my information publishing business.

There is a pattern to creating multiple streams of residual income from the successful examples I have quoted above. You have to learn the base skills in one stream and leverage those skills later to create additional streams. You have to learn to walk with one stream before running with multiple streams of residual income. You have to leverage your existing resources. This concept in the corporate merger world is known as "operating efficiencies." It takes less effort to operate each additional stream of income because they are all built upon the same foundational resources.

If you attempt to create multiple income streams by taking on totally different fields of activity you will be creating mayhem instead of leveraging your resources. This is sure route to failure. If you follow step by step process as outline in this book you will maximize your odds of success.

Practical Steps to Creating Multiple Streams of Residual Income

• **Make a Schedule.** Take time out each day to create residual income. You have to shift from the linear income trap to creating residual income that will someday grow more than your job income. You will not be able to achieve this in a single day. It will take time. Make small changes to your daily schedule to incorporate time for creating residual income. Devote more time each day towards creating residual income as your residual income increases and dependence on linear income goes down. You can only succeed if you target achievable goals, make a schedule and remain focused.

• **Know the Difference between Maintenance Work and Growth Work.** There is no such thing as totally passive income. Every passive income will have some maintenance work. It may not require your day to day involvement but monitoring work will be needed. Even as you carry out maintenance work you should be on lookout for new growth opportunities. Growth work creates multiple income streams.

• **Engage in Only One Growth Activity at a Time.** There is no point dissipating your energy on several growth opportunities simultaneously. You will inch slowly towards these opportunities. It is better to focus on one growth opportunity at a time. Create a successful residual income from it before moving on to another growth activity. You will make money more efficiently by following this simple strategy without overwhelming yourself. Let us say you have 4 growth projects that will take one week each to execute. If you start all of them simultaneously it will take your 4 weeks to complete the projects. If you follow this strategy you will have residual income coming from your projects after 4 weeks. Now let us say you decide to take one project at a time. On completion of the first week you will have one income stream bringing in residual income. At the end of second week another stream of income will go on line and so forth. This is a far superior strategy as you will start generating residual income much quicker without stressing or overwhelming yourself. This is a very simplistic example because it takes much more than a week to start creating a residual income stream.

- **The More the Merrier.** The more residual income streams you create the more financial security you will have. Small trickles will result into a stream and small streams will result into a river someday. Don't discount the little ones. A website may pay you $50 in a year. This is fine as long as it does not take your precious time in maintenance. Your passive income sources can be shares, government bonds, mutual funds, interest earned from bank accounts, blogs, affiliate sales, email marketing, royalties form book sales etc. Each of these can create a small residual income stream for you.

- **Not all Passive Income Streams are Worthwhile.** Not all residual income streams are equal. Some may require more maintenance effort than others. You may require selling some of your income streams if they become irksome. I sell my properties that are difficult to manage or have very little cash flow. By doing so I create time for myself and redeploy the capital into something that can create better residual income for me.

- **Don't Burn Bridges.** You might push aside certain income stream to generate greater efficiency does not mean that you should turn off the tap altogether. Keep monitoring an income stream by visiting it periodically. If the circumstances and economic conditions change then you should be in a position to take advantage of that income stream.

- **Quickest Method of Creating Residual Income is Buying Paper Assets.** If you have some capital sitting idle then buy paper assets that generate highest rate of return. This is the Warren Buffet formula. You buy an asset for cash flow. Capital gain will happen if the asset you have purchased has good management behind it.

- **Generate Multiple Streams of Income Online.** Internet is the fastest and easiest way to generate multiple streams of residual income with least amount of investment and risk. This is because it is very easy to automate your online business. Why most people fail to generate income online is because it is relatively easy to create a website but difficult to drive traffic to it. Without traffic there are no sales. Traffic is the life blood of online residual income. You have to master traffic techniques before you can create a successful online business. So spend some time, effort and money in learning how to generate traffic. Once you master traffic skills then creating multiple streams of income on the internet will become relatively simple. If you are not skilled at generating web traffic then another simple method to generate online residual income is by partnering with companies on profit sharing basis. I have explained this method in detail in my book "**The**

Why Create Multiple Streams of Residual Income?

30 Minute Workweek". This model alone creates a residual income for me on which I can retire. The beauty of this business model is that you have to work less than 5 minutes per day.

Final Thoughts

I simply cannot over emphasize the importance of making a shift from linear income where you trade your hours for money towards creating a residual income where money and systems work for you day in and day out whether you are physically present or not. This is perhaps the most important secret of wealth creation. If you carry one message from this book is that creating residual income is the most important step towards gaining financial freedom.

Creating multiple streams of residual income is a step further and a very desirable objective only if you implement the strategy properly. With little effort you can leverage your existing resources and knowledge to create additional revenue streams. There will be challenges along the way as you will need to shift your thinking and acquire new skills. You will radiate with joy and confidence when you see small streams of income joining into becoming full flow of residual cash flow that will bring prosperity to your family and loved ones for generations to come.

PS: I hope you enjoyed reading the book and found it beneficial. I will appreciate if you will please review the book for benefit of the other readers.

Final Thoughts

Other Books by the Author

- How to Grow Rich with the Power of Compounding
- How to Grow Rich with the Millionaire Mind Script
- How to Grow Rich with the Power of Networking
- How to Grow Rich with the Power of Leverage
- How to Become a Millionaire: Master the Mind Game

About The Author

Praveen Kumar was abandoned by his father at the age of fourteen and joined the Navy at tender age of fifteen where education and free rations were guaranteed.

In order to understand the root cause of suffering he turned towards philosophy and religion. His intense spiritual quest lasted for over fifteen years. During this period he totally neglected the material side of life.

Then one fine day he understood that 'life is 'and material and spiritual world are closely interwoven. You cannot live in one without the other. There is a saying that **'Once your mind expands it never goes back to its original state'**. Something of the sorts happened to him and the transition happened within a very short period of time. His doubts and sufferings vanished and his mind became balanced and steady.

About The Author

One of the reasons he identified as root cause of his suffering was his deep seated financial insecurity resulting from his childhood deprivation. He took premature retirement from the Navy after having successfully commanded submarines and set about building his financial future.

Within short span of a decade starting out with virtually no capital he built his financial empire that has allowed him to retire and work from home.

Praveen strongly feels that it is only through increasing ones spiritual, emotional and financial intelligence can someone transform not only ones own life but also of his loved ones. He now writes books and articles on financial and spiritual matters to empower people to improve their lives.

It was education that changed Praveen's life or how could a boy who was abandoned in a non-descript town in India earn millions and send his children to best schools in USA and New Zealand. It is his mission in life to help educate people in wealth creation as according to him poverty is greatest curse in life that even restricts your emotional and spiritual growth.

Praveen is a **best-selling author** who has helped hundreds of people to get started on their journey to create sustainable wealth with minimum risk. You can visit his http://praveen-kumar.net/ for more information on accelerated wealth creation strategies that will help you obtain financial freedom within a very short time frame.

You can skype Praveen Kumar on
'praveenkumar444'

Made in the USA
Lexington, KY
16 October 2014